A WORLD OF RECIPES

Mexico

REVISED AND UPDATED

Julie McCulloch

Heinemann
LIBRARY

www.heinemannlibrary.co.uk
Visit our website to find out more information about Heinemann Library books.

To order:

☎ Phone +44 (0) 1865 888066

🖷 Fax +44 (0) 1865 314091

🖳 Visit www.heinemannlibrary.co.uk

Heinemann Library is an imprint of Capstone Global Library Limited, a company incorporated in England and Wales having its registered office at 7 Pilgrim Street, London, EC4V 6LB - Registered company number: 6695582

"Heinemann" is a registered trademark of Pearson Education Limited, under licence to Capstone Global Library Limited

Text © Capstone Global Library Limited 2001, 2009
Second edition first published in hardback in 2009
Second edition first published in paperback in 2009
The moral rights of the proprietor have been asserted.

Edited by David Andrews and Diyan Leake
Designed by Richard Parker
Illustrated by Nicholas Beresford-Davis
Picture research by Mica Brancic
Originated by Chroma Graphics (Overseas) Pte Ltd
Printed and bound in China by Leo Paper Products Ltd

ISBN 978 0 431 11815 4 (hardback)
13 12 11 10 09
10 9 8 7 6 5 4 3 2 1

ISBN 978 0 431 11827 7 (paperback)
13 12 11 10 09
10 9 8 7 6 5 4 3 2 1

British Library Cataloguing in Publication Data
McCulloch, Julie, 1973-
   Mexico. - (A world of recipes)
A full catalogue record for this book is available from the British Library.

Acknowledgments
We would like to thank the following for permission to reproduce photographs: © Capstone Global Library Ltd/MM Studios pp. **16**, **17**; Gareth Boden pp. **8–15**, **18–43**; Getty Images (National Geographic/© Gina Martin) p. **7**; © Getty Images p. **5** (Taxi/Ty Allison); Photolibrary Group p. **6** (© SGM SGM).

Cover photograph of tortillas and salsa reproduced with permission of Getty Images (Photographer's Choice/Justin Lightley).

Every effort has been made to contact copyright holders of material reproduced in this book. Any omissions will be rectified in subsequent printings if notice is given to the publishers.

All the Internet addresses (URLs) given in this book were valid at the time of going to press. However, due to the dynamic nature of the Internet, some addresses may have changed, or sites may have changed or ceased to exist since publication. While the author and Publishers regret any inconvenience this may cause readers, no responsibility for any such changes can be accepted by either the author or the Publishers.

Contents

Key: *easy **medium ***difficult

Some words are shown in bold, **like this**. You can find out what they mean by looking in the glossary.

Mexico

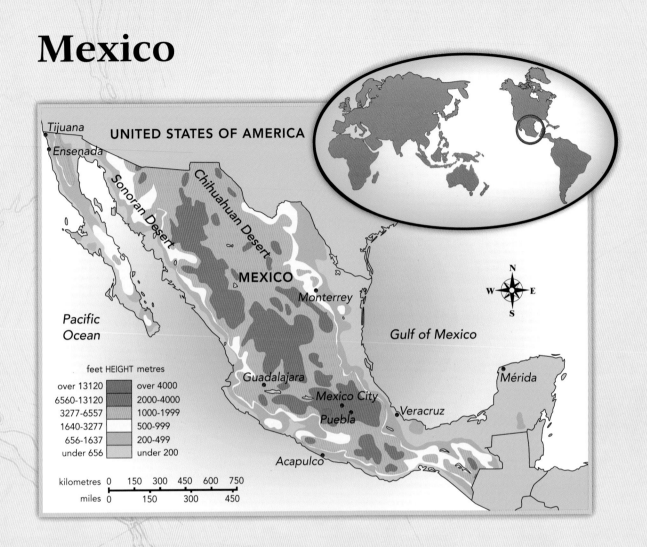

The Republic of Mexico is the eighth largest nation in the world. Mexico has long coastlines on the Pacific Ocean and the Gulf of Mexico. The Sonoran and the Chihuahuan deserts are in the far north. The northern plain, with rolling hills, is home to ranches and farms. The central mountain ranges feature two active volcanoes. Southern Mexico contains flat, marshy land and rainforests.

The climate of Mexico is also diverse. The south is hot and wet, while the north has a milder, drier climate. There may even be snow on the mountain. The weather on the coasts is hot and sometimes humid.

In the past

The Mayans were people who lived in Mexico from 600 to 900 AD. They grew sweetcorn, beans, and squash.

Mayan culture was based on religion with many festivals for the gods. The Mayans built temples shaped like pyramids. Science, mathematics, and astronomy were also important.

The Aztec people (900–1500 AD) came from the north. They created a rich, powerful empire. Their capital city was filled with markets, temples, and floating gardens. This city eventually became Mexico City, the modern capital. An Aztec legend about an eagle eating a snake is shown by an emblem on the Mexican flag.

In the early 16th century, Mexico was conquered by Spain and became known as "New Spain". It remained under Spanish rule until its war of independence began in 1810. Spanish is still the main language spoken in Mexico. The citizens of Mexico are mainly mestizos (a mixture of Spanish and native peoples).

Mexico today

Today, the Roman Catholic religion and family life are important in Mexico. The many holidays include saints' days, when there are church services, parades, fireworks, dancing, and feasting. The Day of the Dead is celebrated after Halloween. It is a time for families to remember loved ones.

At Christmas parties, children break open *piñatas* filled with sweets or toys. Families dress up as Biblical characters and sing carols. Mexicans also celebrate Independence Day. Popular sports throughout the year are bullfighting and football.

↑ *Piñatas* are a fun part of Mexican Christmas celebrations.

Mexican food

Farming has existed in Mexico for over 7000 years. Once maize began to be planted, early tribes abandoned a nomadic hunter-gatherer lifestyle and settled in villages. The Mayans and Aztecs also grew squash, beans, tomatoes, and chilli peppers.

The Spanish introduced European foods including milk, cheese, chicken, and wheat. Ancient foods and Spanish foods blended to create modern Mexican cooking with its bright colours. Many different vegetables and fruits are used, while chillies add spiciness. Maize remains important for making tortillas and tamales (flat breads). Tomatoes and beans are used in stews and soups.

Around the country

Mexico's geography allows a variety of food to be produced. On the northern plains, beef cattle are raised. A wide array of vegetables grow in the cool central mountains.

↑ These pineapples are growing on a plantation in a hot, **tropical** climate.

The hotter areas in the south produce tropical fruit such as papayas, pineapples, and coconuts. Rice is grown extensively in the south-east with its monsoon-type rains. Two crops a year are possible. Most Mexican meals feature a rice dish, either savoury or sweet. Seafood is abundant along the coastlines.

Markets have been an important part of life for centuries. In Aztec markets, cocoa beans were used in payment. Today, towns often have street markets where Mexicans can meet friends and buy their traditional food.

Mexican meals

At breakfast, many Mexicans have coffee with cinnamon and sugar, sweet rolls, and maybe yoghurt. Lunch, or *comida*, is usually the main meal. It often consists of three courses: a starter, a main course, and a pudding.

The early evening meal – *merienda* – is usually a light snack such as cereal, tortillas, and hot chocolate. The day ends with *cena*, a light supper, which can be leftovers from *comida*, a potato and onion omelette, or a sandwich.

Festival foods

Special foods are important at festivals. Fruit drinks are given out by schools and businesses during Lent, the forty days before Easter. During Holy Week (Easter week) ice cream and fruit bars are sold from push-carts. One summer fiesta celebrates the vanilla bean.

The Day of the Dead features bread shaped like dogs, sugar skulls, and chocolate coffins. On this day, people gather in cemeteries for a picnic. To celebrate Independence Day, Mexicans eat green chillies stuffed with meat and spices. Before Christmas, neighbours throw *posadas*, or parties.

↑ A wide variety of chillies can be found in the markets of Mexico.

Ingredients

peppers

avocados

tomatoes

beans

sweetcorn

tortillas

chocolate

chillies

The ingredients for most Mexican dishes are quite easy to find in supermarkets and shops. Here are some of the most common ones.

Avocados

Avocados originally came from Central and South America. The name "avocado" comes from the Mexican word *ahuacatl*. Avocados are a fruit, not a vegetable, and they have a very large stone in the centre.

Beans

Different beans are used in many Mexican recipes. Two of the most common types of beans are butter beans (used in the recipe on page 24) and kidney beans (used in the recipe on page 28). They are easiest to use if you buy them in cans.

Chillies

Chillies are spicy peppers used in many Mexican dishes. There are hundreds of different sorts – some are quite mild, and others are very, very hot! Fresh chillies contain an oil that can make your eyes and skin sting if it touches them, so it is a good idea to use chilli powder, made from ground-up dried chillies, rather than fresh ones. If you don't like spicy food, just leave out the chilli powder.

Chocolate

Chocolate has been eaten and drunk in Mexico for thousands of years. It is made from the roasted, crushed beans of the cocoa plant. In Mexico, chocolate is made into hot drinks, used in puddings, and used in savoury sauces. Plain, dark chocolate is the best sort to use in Mexican recipes.

Sweetcorn

Sweetcorn was one of the first plants grown in Mexico, and it is used in many dishes. You can buy sweetcorn fresh on the cob (either in its leafy case or with this stripped off), frozen on the cob, or separated from the cob (frozen or canned).

Tomatoes

Tomatoes are used in many Mexican recipes. You can use either fresh or canned tomatoes in the recipes in this book.

Tortillas

Tortillas are flat circles of bread. They are eaten with many different meals in Mexico. Two different types of tortillas are eaten in Mexico – wheat tortillas (which contain wheat flour) and corn tortillas (which contain flour made from ground sweetcorn). Sweetcorn flour can be difficult to find, so the recipe for tortillas in this book is for wheat tortillas.

Before you start

Which recipe should I try?

The recipes you choose to make depends on many things. Some recipes make a good main course, while others are better as starters. Some are easy, others are more difficult.

The top right-hand page of each recipe has information that can help you. It tells you how long each recipe will take and how many people it serves. You can multiply or divide the quantities if you want to cook for more or fewer people. This section also shows how difficult each dish is to make: the recipes are easy (*), medium (**), or difficult (***) to cook. The symbols in the corner can help you quickly find certain recipes. Here is a key that will help you.

Healthy choice: These recipes are healthy to eat.

Quick and easy: These recipes are quick and easy to make.

Sweet treat: These recipes make a good dessert or sweet snack.

This symbol ⚠ is sign of a dangerous step in a recipe. For these steps, take extra care or ask an adult to help.

Kitchen rules

There are a few basic rules you should always follow when you cook:

- Ask an adult if you can use the kitchen.
- Wash your hands before you start.
- Wear an apron to protect your clothes. Tie back long hair.
- Be very careful when using sharp knives.
- Never leave pan handles sticking out – it could be dangerous if you bump into them.
- Always wear oven gloves to lift things in and out of the oven.
- Wash fruit and vegetables before you use them.

Quantities and measurements

Ingredients for recipes can be measured in two different ways. Metric measurements use grams, litres, and millilitres. Imperial measurements use cups, ounces, and fluid ounces. In the recipes in this book you will see the following abbreviations:

tbsp = tablespoons   oz = ounces
tsp = teaspoons   ml = millilitres
g = grams   cm = centimetres

Utensils

To cook the recipes in this book, you will need these utensils, as well as kitchen essentials such as forks, spoons, plates, and bowls.

- baking tin
- baking tray
- chopping board
- foil
- food processor or blender
- frying pan
- grater
- large, flat, ovenproof dish
- heatproof bowl
- measuring jug
- potato masher
- rolling pin
- saucepan with lid
- set of scales
- sharp knife
- sieve or **colander**
- whisk
- wooden cocktail sticks

Tortillas

Tortillas are eaten with many Mexican meals. Sometimes they are served as an accompaniment to the meal, but often they form part of the meal itself, usually by being wrapped around different fillings.

The recipes for cheese-filled enchiladas (page 22) and fish burritos (page 30) use tortillas, so you will need to make some tortillas before cooking these dishes. You can also buy ready-made tortillas, but here is how to make your own.

What you need

100g plain flour
  (+ a few extra tbsp
  to sprinkle on the
  chopping board)
1 tsp salt
2 tbsp olive oil
4 tbsp warm water

What you do

1 Put the flour and salt into a mixing bowl. Mix in the oil with a spoon, then gradually stir in the warm water until the mixture starts to form a **dough**.

2 **Sprinkle** some flour onto a chopping board. **Knead** the dough on the board until it is smooth.

3 Divide the dough into four pieces, to make four tortillas.

4 Shape one piece of dough into a ball, then flatten it.

5 Sprinkle some more flour onto the board and onto a rolling pin. Roll out the ball of dough into a circle, until the dough is as thin as you can make it without breaking it.

6 Heat a frying pan until it sizzles when you sprinkle a drop of water into it. Put the tortilla into the pan.

7 Cook the tortilla for one minute, then turn it over and cook the other side for 30 seconds. Slide the cooked tortilla out of the pan onto a plate.

8 Repeat steps 4 to 7 with the other three pieces of dough.

STORING TORTILLAS

You can store your tortillas to use later. Put a square of **greaseproof paper** between each tortilla so that they don't stick together. Leave them to cool, then put the stack of tortillas into a plastic bag. They will keep for several days in the fridge.

Guacamole

Guacamole is eaten all over Mexico. It can be eaten as a snack, spread on tortillas, or used as an accompaniment to other dishes.

What you need

1 onion
A handful of fresh coriander leaves (see box on next page)
¼ tsp chilli powder (optional)
1 avocado
1 tbsp lemon juice

What you do

1. **Peel** the skin from the onion, and finely **chop** half of it.

2. Finely chop the fresh coriander.

3. In a bowl, mix together the chopped onion, coriander and chilli powder (if you are using it).

4. Cut the avocado in half lengthways. Use a spoon to remove the stone.

5. Use the spoon to scoop out the flesh of the avocado into the bowl, leaving the skin behind.

6. Add the lemon juice to the mixture.

7. **Mash** all the ingredients together with a fork.

CORIANDER

Coriander is a herb that looks a bit like parsley. It is used a lot in Mexican cooking. You will usually find fresh coriander in the fruit and vegetable section of supermarkets. If you can't find any, try using fresh parsley leaves instead. Don't substitute dried coriander, though. This is made from the seeds, rather than the leaves, of the coriander plant, and tastes completely different!

Cornbread

Mexican cornbread is a sweet-tasting bread that is easy to make. It is often served up at meal times in Mexican households. The bread gets its name from the cornmeal that is used as one of the primary ingredients in making it. Other flours made from maize, such as polenta, can also be used to make cornbread, although it won't taste quite like the real thing.

What you need

- 120g plain flour
- 120g fine cornmeal or polenta
- 1 tbsp baking powder
- ½ tsp salt
- 2 eggs
- 300ml semi-skimmed milk
- 50g butter
- 200g tinned sweetcorn
- ¼ tsp chilli powder (optional)

What you do

1 Lightly **grease** a baking tin.

2 **Preheat** the oven to 200°C/400°F/gas mark 6.

3 Combine the flour, cornmeal or polenta, baking powder, and salt in a mixing bowl.

4 **Beat** the eggs with the milk in another bowl.

5 **Melt** the butter and add it to the eggs and milk.

6 **Drain** and rinse the sweetcorn and mix it with the eggs, along with the chilli powder, if using. Add the egg mixture to the dry ingredients and stir to a smooth batter.

7 Pour the mixture into the prepared tin. **Bake** for 20–25 minutes until golden brown, firm, and beginning to pull away from the sides of the tin.

8 Cut into pieces while still warm and serve straight away.

Corn soup

Hot soup is often served in the cold, mountainous regions of Mexico. Most lunches start with a bowl of soup, and many evening meals consist of soup served with a stack of tortillas. This simple corn soup is full of flavour and very **nourishing**.

If you use the frozen sweetcorn, you need to **thaw** it before you use it. You can do this in two ways:

a) take it out of the freezer at least an hour before you want to use it, and leave it to stand;

b) pour hot water over the sweetcorn, leave it to stand for a couple of minutes, then carefully empty the sweetcorn into a **colander** or sieve to **drain**.

What you need

1 onion
1 red pepper
400ml water
1 tbsp sunflower oil
225g canned or
    frozen sweetcorn
1 vegetable stock cube
125ml plain natural
    yoghurt

What you do

1 **Peel** the skin from the onion, and finely **chop** half of it.

2 Cut the red pepper in half, then scoop out the seeds. Chop half of the flesh into strips.

3 Put the water into a saucepan, and bring it to the **boil**. Crumble the stock cube into the water, and stir until it **dissolves**. Put the stock to one side.

4 Heat the oil in a saucepan. **Fry** the chopped onion and red pepper for about 5 minutes.

5 Put the onion and pepper mixture and the sweetcorn into a blender or food processor. **Blend** until smooth.

6 Put the mixture back into the saucepan, and add the stock.

7 **Simmer** the soup for about 5 minutes, until it is hot.

8 Stir in the yoghurt. You can use the other half of the red pepper to **garnish** your soup.

COLD SOUP

This dish can also be served cold for a refreshing summer soup. Let the soup cool, then put it into the fridge for a couple of hours before serving it.

Grilled corn on the cob with salsa

Corn on the cob can be eaten on its own or with a sauce. This recipe shows you how to make corn on the cob with salsa, which is a spicy Mexican sauce made with tomatoes and fruit. Mexican people eat salsa with many different dishes. In Mexican restaurants, you often find a bowl of salsa on the table along with the salt and pepper.

What you need

- 1 onion
- 2 tomatoes
- 1 red pepper
- 1 slice of canned pineapple
- 2 cobs of sweetcorn
- 2 tbsp sunflower oil
- 2 tsp chilli powder (optional)

What you do

1. **Peel** the onion and finely **chop** half of it.

2. Chop the tomatoes into small pieces.

3. Cut the red pepper in half, then scoop the seeds out. Chop half of the flesh into strips.

4. Chop the slice of pineapple into small pieces.

5. Heat 1 tbsp of the oil in a saucepan over a medium heat. Add the chopped onion and the chilli powder (if you are using any). **Fry** for 5 minutes, or until the onion is soft.

6. Add the chopped tomatoes, red pepper, and pineapple. Turn the heat down to low, and **cover** the pan. Leave the salsa to **simmer** for about 10 minutes, stirring occasionally.

Ready to eat: 35 minutes. Difficulty: **. Serves 2.

7 While the salsa is cooking, brush the remaining 1 tbsp of oil onto the sweetcorn.

8 Put the sweetcorn on a baking tray and **grill** them for about 10 minutes, turning them occasionally so they are cooked on all sides.

9 Put the sweetcorn onto plates, and spoon half of the salsa sauce onto each plate.

HOT AND SALTY

For a really quick snack, try making corn on the cob with butter and salt. Grill the sweetcorn as described above, then spread butter on them while they are still hot, so it melts into the corn. **Sprinkle** them with salt, and eat them straight away. Take care they don't burn the inside of your mouth, though!

Cheese-filled enchiladas

Enchiladas are tortillas rolled around a filling. These cheesy enchiladas are served with a hot tomato sauce.

What you need

For the tomato sauce:
1 onion
1 clove of garlic
150g tomatoes
1 tbsp sunflower oil

For the filling:
100g half-fat hard cheese (for example, Cheddar)
250g cottage cheese

4 tortillas (bought or home-made – see pages 12–13)

What you do

1 **Preheat** the oven to 190°C/ 375°F/gas mark 5.

2 **Peel** the onion and the garlic, and finely **chop** them.

3 Chop the tomatoes into small pieces.

4 Heat the oil in a frying pan. **Fry** the onion and garlic on a low heat for 5 minutes, or until the onion is soft, but not brown.

5 Add the chopped tomatoes. **Cover** the pan and **simmer** the mixture for about 20 minutes, stirring occasionally.

DIFFERENT FILLINGS
You can make enchiladas with all sorts of different fillings. Here are some ideas:
- guacamole (see page 14)
- picadillo (see page 26)
- chilli con carne (see page 28)

6 While the tomato sauce is simmering, **grate** the hard cheese. Mix ⅔ of the hard cheese with all of the cottage cheese in a bowl. (Keep the rest of the hard cheese for later.)

7 Place 2 tbsp of the cheese mixture onto each tortilla, then roll it into a tube.

8 Put the rolled-up tortillas into a large, flat, ovenproof dish.

9 Pour the tomato sauce over the rolled-up tortillas, then **sprinkle** the remaining hard cheese over the top.

10 Cover the dish with foil, and **bake** in the oven for 30 minutes. Remove the foil and bake for a further 15 minutes until the cheese is brown and bubbling.

Bean and potato patties

Beans are eaten in many different ways in Mexico. These bean and potato patties are good served with spicy salsa (see recipe on page 20).

What you need

250g potatoes
60g half-fat hard cheese (for example, Cheddar)
1 egg
125g canned butter beans
2 tbsp flour
½ tbsp sunflower oil

What you do

1. Carefully **peel** the potatoes using a sharp knife, then cut them into small pieces.

2. Put the potatoes into a saucepan full of water, and **boil** them for about 15 minutes until they are soft.

3. While the potatoes are boiling, **grate** the cheese into a small bowl.

4. Crack the egg into a bowl. **Beat** it with a fork or a whisk until the yolk and the white are mixed.

5. When the potatoes are soft, **drain** them by emptying the pan into a **colander** or sieve. Put the drained potatoes back into the pan.

6. Drain the butter beans and put them into the pan with the potatoes. **Mash** the potatoes and beans together with a fork or a potato masher.

7. Add the grated cheese and beaten egg to the mashed potatoes and beans. Mix everything together well.

8. Divide the mixture into four pieces, and shape each piece into a flattened round patty.

 **9** **Sprinkle** the flour onto a chopping board. Turn the patties over a couple of times on the board to coat them in flour.

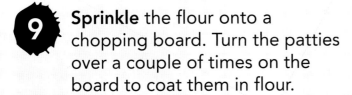 **10** Heat the oil in a frying pan over a low heat. Put the patties into the pan, and **fry** them gently for 10 minutes. Turn them over carefully, and fry on the other side for another 10 minutes.

Picadillo

Picadillo is a main course dish made from minced beef, fruit, and spices. It is usually served with long grain rice or tortillas.

What you need

½ onion
1 clove of garlic
1 apple
1 tbsp sunflower oil
150g tomatoes
200g minced beef
¼ tsp chilli powder (optional)
25g raisins
½ tsp cinnamon
½ tsp cumin

What you do

1 **Peel** the onion and the garlic, and **chop** them finely.

2 Using a sharp knife, carefully cut the apple into pieces. Don't use the core of the apple.

3 Chop the tomatoes into small pieces.

4 Heat the oil in a frying pan over a medium heat. Add the minced beef, the onion, and the garlic.

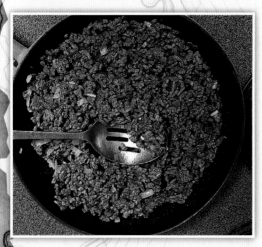

5 **Fry** the mixture for 15 minutes, stirring occasionally, until the onion is soft and the beef is brown.

6 Add the apple, tomatoes, chilli powder (if using any), raisins, cinnamon, and cumin to the pan.

7 **Cover** the pan and cook the picadillo over a low heat for about 15 minutes, stirring occasionally.

PICADILLO-STUFFED PEPPERS

Picadillo is sometimes served stuffed into red peppers. This looks impressive, but is easy to do! Carefully cut the top off a red pepper, and scoop out the seeds. Spoon the cooked picadillo into the hollow pepper, replace the pepper's top, and bake in an oven at 180°C/ 350°F/gas mark 4 for about 40 minutes.

27

Chilli con carne

Chilli con carne means "chillies with meat". Chillies are an important part of many Mexican dishes. In the past, Mexican people believed that chillies could cure many illnesses, including toothache and ear-ache. Modern science has proved that chillies do contain lots of healthy **vitamins**. Serve chilli con carne with long grain rice.

What you need

1 tbsp sunflower oil
200g lean minced beef
1 onion
1 clove of garlic
½ tsp chilli powder (optional)
150g tomatoes
80g canned kidney beans

What you do

1 **Preheat** the oven to 160°C/ 325°F/gas mark 3.

2 **Peel** the skin from the onion and the garlic clove, and finely **chop** them.

3 Chop the tomatoes into small pieces.

4 Heat the oil in a frying pan over a medium heat. Add the chopped onion and garlic and the minced beef.

5 **Fry** the mixture for about 15 minutes, stirring occasionally to stop it from sticking.

6 Add the chilli powder (if you are using any), chopped tomatoes, and **drained** kidney beans to the pan.

7 Cook the mixture for another 5 minutes, then pour it carefully into an ovenproof dish.

8 **Cover** the dish, and cook your chilli con carne in the oven for 1 hour.

9 Put the cooked chilli in a serving bowl. You can also serve chilli with tortillas.

VEGETARIAN CHILLI

You can make a **vegetarian** version of this dish, called *chilli sin carne* – chillies without meat! Just replace the minced beef with chopped vegetables, such as courgettes, mushrooms, and red peppers.

Fish burritos

These are little parcels of fish, wrapped in tortillas. They are delicious served with guacamole (see recipe on page 14). You can use fresh or frozen fish for this recipe, but make sure frozen fish is well **thawed**.

What you need

For the filling:
1 onion
2 fish fillets (thawed if frozen)
½ tbsp sunflower oil
¼ tsp chilli powder (optional)
50ml plain natural yogurt

4 tortillas (bought or home-made – see pages 12–13)
60g half-fat hard cheese (for example, Cheddar)

What you do

1 **Preheat** the oven to 180°C/350°F/gas mark 4.

2 **Peel** the onion and finely **chop** half of it.

3 Put the fish into a saucepan. Just cover it with water, bring to the **boil**, and then **simmer** for 5 minutes.

4 **Drain** the water from the fish. Use a fork to **flake** it into a bowl, making sure you take out the skin and any bones.

 5 Heat the oil in a frying pan over a medium heat. **Fry** the chopped onion and chilli powder (if you are using any) for 5 minutes, until the onion is soft. Add this mixture to the fish.

6 Add the yoghurt to the fish and onions, and mix well.

7 Put a couple of spoonfuls of the fish mixture on to each tortilla, then fold the tortilla to make a parcel. Use cocktail sticks through each parcel to keep it closed.

8 Put the parcels into an ovenproof dish.

9 **Grate** the cheese over the parcels. **Cover** the dish with foil and **bake** for 30 minutes.

10 Remove the cocktail sticks before serving.

Mexican rice

This rice dish is **nourishing** enough to serve as a main course on its own. There are two different types of rice – long and short grain. This dish works best made with long grain rice.

What you need

½ onion
1 clove of garlic
150g tomatoes
300ml water
1 vegetable stock cube
1 tbsp sunflower oil
125g rice
½ tsp chilli powder (optional)
60g frozen peas

What you do

1 **Peel** the onion and garlic, and finely **chop** them.

2 Chop the tomatoes into small pieces.

3 Put the water into a saucepan, and bring it to the **boil**. Crumble the stock cube into the water, and stir until it **dissolves**. Put the stock to one side.

4 Heat the oil in a saucepan over a medium heat. Add the onions, garlic, and rice, and cook for 5 minutes, stirring all the time to stop the rice from sticking.

5 Add the tomatoes, stock, chilli powder (if you are using any), and peas to the pan. Bring to the boil, then reduce the heat to low.

6 **Cover** the pan and **simmer** for about 20 minutes, stirring occasionally, until all the liquid has been soaked up.

HEALTHY EXTRAS

In some regions of Mexico, rice and beans are eaten at nearly every meal. Rice and beans are both cheap ingredients that provide a great deal of nourishment – **protein** from the beans and **carbohydrate** from the rice.

Savoury fruit salad

You can serve this salad with many of the dishes in this book. It goes well with meat dishes such as picadillo and chilli con carne.

What you need

- 1 small lettuce
- 1 carrot
- 1 apple
- 2 slices of canned pineapple
- 1 banana
- 1 orange
- 2 tbsp lemon juice
- 2 tbsp sunflower oil

What you do

 Cut or the **shred** the lettuce leaves, and put them into a salad bowl.

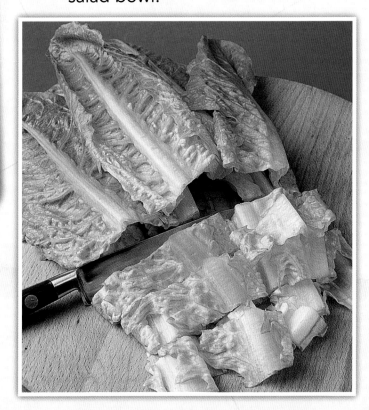

2 Carefully wash the carrot and **grate** it into the salad bowl.

3 Cut the apple into small pieces. Don't use the core of the apple. Add the apple pieces to the salad bowl.

4 **Chop** the pineapple slices into small pieces, and add them to the salad bowl.

5 **Peel** the banana, then chop it into slices and add these to the bowl.

6 Peel the orange, and divide it into segments. Add these to the salad.

7 In a small bowl, mix the lemon juice and the oil. Pour this mixture over the salad as a **dressing**.

8 Mix, or **toss**, the salad well just before you serve it.

Rice pudding

Rice pudding is made in many different countries. This fruity Mexican version is very easy to make. There are two different sorts of rice – long and short grain. This dish works best with short grain rice, which is often called 'pudding rice' in shops.

What you need

- 50g rice
- 125ml water
- 225ml milk
- 100g granulated sugar
- 40g raisins
- ½ tsp cinnamon
- 10g butter

What you do

1 Put the rice into a saucepan and add the water. Bring it to the **boil**, then turn the heat down to low.

2 **Cover** the pan and **simmer** for about 20 minutes, until the rice has soaked up all the water and is soft.

3 Add the milk, sugar, raisins, and cinnamon to the pan and stir everything together.

4 Cook the rice pudding over a low heat, stirring all the time, until all the milk has been soaked up. This should take about 5 minutes.

5 Stir the butter into the hot rice pudding until it **melts**, then serve.

ADDED EXTRAS

This rice pudding tastes really good served with fruit. You could try arranging a few segments of orange or some slices of apple alongside the rice pudding when you serve it.

Cinnamon oranges

Many Mexican farmers grow oranges. This refreshing dessert is very easy to make.

What you need

2 oranges
25g caster sugar
¼ tsp ground cinnamon

What you do

1 **Peel** the skin from the oranges, then **slice** them thinly.

2 Place the oranges in a serving bowl.

3 Mix the sugar and the cinnamon together in a small bowl, then **sprinkle** them over the oranges.

4 Put the oranges, sugar, and cinnamon in the fridge for at least 1 hour before serving, to **chill** them.

MEXICAN DESSERTS

Puddings and other sweet things are very popular in Mexico. Some of the most popular desserts are made from fresh fruit, often served with spices and sugar or honey, as in this dish.

Ready to eat: 1 hour 15 minutes (including 1 hour to chill the oranges). Difficulty: *. Serves 2.

MEXICAN MARKETS
Many Mexican people buy their fruit and vegetables from street markets. Most Mexican towns have a market day, or *dia del mercado*. Markets are a good place not only to shop, but also to meet people.

Caramel custard

A version of caramel custard is made in many countries around the world. In Mexico, this dish is called *flan*. It was probably brought to Mexico by the Spanish conquerors in the 16th century, and is now a firm favourite. This dish needs time to **chill** in the fridge, so make it several hours before you want to eat it.

What you need

2 eggs
60g caster sugar
1 tbsp water
225ml semi-skimmed milk
A few drops of vanilla essence

What you do

1 **Preheat** the oven to 150°C/ 300°F/gas mark 2.

2 Crack the eggs into a bowl. **Beat** them with a fork or a **whisk** until the yolk and the white are mixed.

3 Put half the sugar into a saucepan and add the water. Put the saucepan over a low heat and stir gently until all the sugar has **dissolved**.

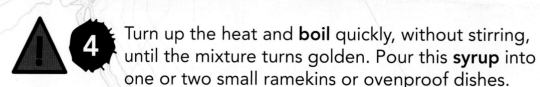

4 Turn up the heat and **boil** quickly, without stirring, until the mixture turns golden. Pour this **syrup** into one or two small ramekins or ovenproof dishes.

5 Heat the milk in a saucepan over a medium heat. Add the rest of the sugar and the vanilla **essence**. Heat for another 3 minutes, until the sugar has dissolved.

6 Let the milk **cool** down slightly, then stir the beaten eggs into it. Pour the mixture on top of the syrup and put the ramekins into a large ovenproof dish. Carefully pour hot water around them until the water reaches about halfway up their sides.

Ready to eat: 4 hours (including 3 hours to chill the custard).
Difficulty: ***. Serves 2.

7 **Cover** the ovenproof dish with foil, then put it in the oven and **bake** for 45 minutes.

8 Take the ovenproof dish out of the oven. Lift the hot ramekins of custard out of the ovenproof dish.

9 Leave the custard to cool, then put it into the fridge for at least 3 hours.

10 Dip the bottom of the ramekins into hot water to loosen the custard. Run a knife round the edge of the ramekins.

11 Quickly turn the custard out on to a plate before serving.

Mexican hot chocolate

The combination of plain chocolate, cinnamon, and vanilla is typically Mexican. In fact, Mexican chocolate bars often have cinnamon and vanilla already added to them.

What you need

125g plain chocolate, broken into chunks

400ml water

500ml milk

½ tsp ground cinnamon

A few drops of vanilla essence

What you do

1 You will either need a heatproof bowl that fits on top of your saucepan or you can **melt** the chocolate in the microwave, in a non-metallic, microwave-proof bowl.

2 Break the chocolate into pieces, and put it into your bowl. Then follow either step 3a or step 3b.

3a Put the water into a saucepan. Heat it over a medium heat until just bubbling at the edges but not **boiling**. Reduce the heat to low. Put the bowl of chocolate on top and leave until melted (about 5 minutes).

3b Alternatively, cook the chocolate on medium power in the microwave for 1 minute and 20 seconds and stir until melted.

4 Warm the milk in a small saucepan. Slowly stir half the milk into the melted chocolate.

 Pour the chocolate mixture back into the saucepan with the rest of the milk. Stir in the cinnamon and vanilla **essence**. Heat for a few more minutes.

6 Pour the hot chocolate into cups.

COLD CHOCOLATE

You can also use this recipe to make a cold chocolate drink. Leave the hot chocolate to cool, then whisk it with a fork or whisk before pouring it into cups.

BREAKFAST BREAD

Hot chocolate is often drunk for breakfast in Mexico. It is sometimes accompanied by pan de yema, a type of bread cooked in egg yolks, which is dipped into the hot chocolate.

Further information

Here are some places to find out more about Mexico and Mexican cooking.

Books

Cooking the Mexican Way by Rosa Coronado (Lerner, 2008)

Foods of Mexico by Barbara Sheen (KidHaven Press, 2005)

Funky Chicken Enchiladas: And Other Mexican Dishes by Nick Fauchald (Capstone, 2009)

Mexican Cookbook by Yvette Garfield and Cricket Azima (Handstand Kids, 2008)

The Second International Cookbook for Kids by Matthew Locricchio (Marshall Cavendish, 2008)

The Young Chef's Mexican Cookbook by Karen Ward (Crabtree, 2008)

A Visit to Mexico by Rob Alcraft (Heinemann Library, 2008)

Websites

www.dltk-kids.com/recipesdb/viewbycourse.asp?cid=13

http://kids-cooking.suite101.com/article.cfm/mexican_recipes_kids_can_make

www.circletimekids.com/WorldLibrary/countries/Mexico/recipes

www.kids-cooking-activities.com/Mexican-cooking.html

www.recipeathome.info/Kids.html

Healthy eating

This diagram shows the types and proportion of food you should eat to stay healthy. Eat plenty of foods from the *bread, rice, potatoes, pasta* group and plenty from the *fruit and vegetables* group. Eat some foods from the *milk and dairy* group and the *meat, fish, eggs, beans* group. Foods from the smallest group are not necessary for a healthy diet so eat these in small amounts or only occasionally.

Mexican cooking uses many ingredients from the two largest food groups. Rice and tortillas are from the bread, rice, potatoes, pasta group. People also eat lots of different kinds of vegetables and beans, so you can see how healthy Mexican cooking is!

↑ The Eatwell food plate shows the proportion of food from each food group you should eat to achieve a healthy, balanced diet. This takes account of everything you eat, including snacks.

Glossary

bake cook something in the oven

beat mix something together strongly using a fork, spoon, or whisk

blend mix ingredients together in a blender or food processor

boil cook a liquid on the hob. Boiling liquid bubbles and steams strongly.

carbohydrate food that contains sugar and starch, such as potatoes, which gives us energy

chill put something in the fridge to make it cold before serving it

chop cut something into pieces using a knife

colander bowl-shaped container with holes in it, used for draining vegetables and straining

cool allow hot food to become cold. You should always allow food to cool before putting it in the fridge.

cover put a lid on a pan, or foil over a dish

dissolve mix something into a liquid until it disappears

dough soft mixture of flour and liquid that sticks together and can be shaped or rolled out

drain remove liquid, usually by pouring something into a colander or sieve

dressing oil and vinegar sauce for salad

essence very strong flavouring, such as vanilla or almond essence. It is important not to confuse it with extract – you need only a small drop of essence, while you may need a teaspoonful of extract.

flake break something such as a piece of fish into small pieces

fry cook something in oil in a pan

garnish decorate food – for example, with fresh herbs or lemon wedges

grate break something such as cheese into small pieces, using a grater

grease rub fat over a surface to stop food sticking to it

greaseproof paper kind of paper that does not absorb oil or fat

grill cook something under the grill

knead keep pressing and pushing dough with your hands so that it becomes very soft and stretchy

mash crush something such as potatoes until it is soft and pulpy

melt change from solid to liquid when heated

nourishing good for our bodies and our health

peel remove the skin of a fruit or vegetable

preheat turn on the oven or grill in advance, so that it is hot when you are ready to use it

protein a body building material found in some foods, such as beans, eggs, and meat

shred cut or tear something such as lettuce into small pieces

simmer cook a liquid on the hob. Simmering liquid bubbles and steams gently.

slice cut something into thin, flat pieces

sprinkle scatter small pieces or drops on to something

syrup thick, sweet liquid made from sugar and water

thaw defrost something that has been frozen

toss turn the leaves in a salad over a few times so they are coated in dressing

tropical a hot, wet climate

vegetarian food that does not contain meat or fish. People who don't eat meat or fish are called vegetarians.

vitamin natural chemicals in food that the body uses to stay healthy

whisk mix ingredients using a whisk

Index